Get Into the Zone

The Essential Guide to High Performance Through Mental Training

By Kate Allgood

Praise for *Get Into the Zone*

"Kate Allgood author of "Get into the Zone" has spent her life helping others perform better weather it's in sports or in life. It all starts with our minds. This is a step by step guideline to improving our thoughts to overcome any situation. Self-awareness is a topic that always can be improved. I feel very fortunate I had a chance to work with Kate during my career. Selfishly, I wish Kate came into my life at an earlier time."

— Geoff Geary
Retired Major League Pitcher

"Hats off to Kate Allgood and this amazing book on the power of Sport Psychology. As a life-long athlete myself, I live and breathe the principals that she teaches throughout this book not just on the field but also in my business. I would not be where I am today without Kate's teachings which help me to get through mental hurdles that I face as an entrepreneur.

In sports and in business, the biggest challenge you face is not your competitor, but what is going on in your own mind. Kate shows you specific strategies to get in the zone and kick butt on a daily basis. Just the chapter on Imagery is worth the investment in this book. No matter if you're a top-class athlete or a driven entrepreneur, this book will help you take your mental game to the next level."

— Chris Martinez
CEO/Co-Founder WebsiteIn5Days.com

"I had the pleasure to coach Kate and witness her climb to being the best player in Canada at the University level. Kate was a special player who meshed her hockey and mental skills to make an impact that were evident in practice and transferred into game situations. I highly recommend following what she has written to any athlete that has the desire to become more of a complete, well-rounded, high-performance athlete."

— Todd Erskine
Coordinator Baseball Programs Jays Care Foundation Toronto Blue Jays

"I met Kate at my kickboxing gym and the moment our training session started I knew she had the edge.

Not only did she have the physical edge, she had the mental edge. What makes Kate different is that she was once the athlete who needed someone to help them get than mental edge. She has been through almost everything that today's young athlete experiences in their growing process.

I have had several opportunities to listen and watch Kate speak to athletes and she really knows how to get to them in ways they can understand. I am excited for her as she now gets to spread her knowledge to all athletes and I know she will have a BIG IMPACT!"

— Joseph Virga
Owner/Performance Coach Parisi Speed School San Diego

"Working with Kate has been the best thing for my career and me. Before working with Kate, I had issues that I had no clue that weren't allowing me to flourish on and off the Football field. I had a hard time focusing and it was impacting me on and off the field and I didn't even notice it. Having Kate as a Sport Psychology Coach really helped me to learn how to get in my zone no matter where I was or what I was doing. I went from being just a player on my team, to a vocal leader and a dominant player. I went from a good student to an excellent student. I even learned the best way to be efficient that worked for me, which is very critical as a student athlete.

After finishing my sessions with Kate, many of my peers sensed a change in me. My coaches thought highly of me and said that my performance was far more consistent than it had ever been. My grade point average went from 2.8 to a 3.3 and I completed my college career with a degree in Journalism. I am currently a Freelance Journalist for Kicksonfire.com while I am also training for the National Football League and Canadian Football League.

I know that without working with Kate the results may have not been as good as they were this past season. As a Football player, I recommend this book to anybody. Many of the techniques that I have learned have benefitted me in sports, in the classroom, and in my relationships. If it has worked for me I am certain that it will do the same for you."

— Nate McLaurin
Former College Football Player

"Kate Allgood's short and concise guiding book for high performers on how to "get into the zone" is a very helpful text in sport psychology. It delineates the going forward processes and procedures for athletes and others for obtaining developmental flows and successes in reaching and realizing their highest individual and relational (team) potentials.

It is also a book on advising athletes and other high performers about diverse tempting traps to avoid but first and foremost the author, who is now counseling high performing clients, shares her personal experiences of having had successes as an athlete. She calls upon the readers to explore, find and experiment with the suitable and attractive example and guiding principles in the book, trying them out for themselves.

This humble request from the author for the reader to understand that there is no greater driving force in the performer's life than him/herself creates an authentic trust in the text stemming from the author's own dearly bought experiences of performing.

Last but not least she also puts forward some wise guiding principles about helpful communication between the parents and their child athletes in the preparation, observation and follow up of their performances."

— Ragnvald Kvalsund, Ph.D
Professor of Counselling Department of
Adult Learning and Counselling
The Norwegian University of
Science and Technology Trondheim, Norway

"As a doctor who treats professional athletes weekend warriors and working professionals I can appreciate the need for people to "get into the zone" in their lives . . . whether it be for athletics or for their careers.

Kate does a good job of explaining how one can get into the zone to perform their best, and why sport psychology is a growing and integral part of today's sports culture. The techniques that she discusses to become actively aware and develop positive rituals are some of the things that I see my Elite professional athletes do as they prepare to perform.

Imagery, mental preparation, finding your motivation, and maximizing your potential are some of the important things that Kate discusses in this book. This is an easy read for any athlete, parent or coach looking to understand how our minds work when performing under pressure and for those looking to maximize their edge.

In my sports medicine practice I treat and counsel athletes daily . . . I will be recommending this book as a must read for many of my athletes so that they may be more at ease in pressure situations and have a better understanding of how they can perform their best."

— Dr. Pawen Dhokal, D.C.
Owner Elite Health

"My name is James Langley, former Division I pitcher in the Colonial League for the Drexel Dragons, PLNU GSAC Champions NAIA World Series (ranked 3rd) and Northwoods league standout for the Duluth Huskies. I currently serve on the Board of directors for Big Brothers Big Sisters of San Diego and the Alumni in Business for Point Loma Nazarene. I only reference my past participation in the programs above to help validate my endorsement of Kate Allgood and her book Get Into the Zone.

As a former collegiate/semi professional athlete and most importantly former coach, I cannot fully express the difficulty young athletes face to focus and contribute to their sport without the fear of failure. Sports psychology was the toughest thing for me to develop as a young athlete, and mostly because it simply wasn't discussed. Too much pressure is put on young athletes these days, especially with the specialized focus on certain sports and unwarranted pressure placed by outside sources.

If I could have learned the key factors of the ingredients in Kate's book when I was a young athlete, there is no doubt in my mind I would have achieved greater success and much faster. As an advocate for youth mentoring, I think this book could change many lives of young athletes and many coaches who have an effect on young athletes."

—James Langley
Partner—Schwartz Commercial Realty

Get Into the Zone

The Essential Guide to High Performance Through Mental Training

By Kate Allgood

GET INTO THE ZONE
THE ESSENTIAL GUIDE TO HIGH
PERFORMANCE THROUGH MENTAL TRAINING

Copyright 2015 Quantum Performance Inc
All rights reserved. No part of this book may be reproduced or transmitted in any form or by any means whatsoever without express written permission from the author, except in the case of brief quotations embodied in critical articles and reviews. Please refer all pertinent questions to the publisher.

Contact the Author
www.qpathlete.com

ISBN-13: 978-1511873543
ISBN-10: 151187354X

Table of Contents

Introduction 1
    Who I Am 1
    Why I'm Writing This Book... 3
    Challenges That I See in the World of Sports and Other High End Pursuits 5
    Barriers That I See in Clients That Prevent Them from "Getting into the Zone".. 8
    Purpose of the book 10

Chapter 1: What Does "Getting into the Zone" Mean? 11
    Defining "the Zone" 11
    The Benefits of "Getting into the Zone" 13
    Why it is Hard to "Get into the Zone" 14

Chapter 2: What is Sport Psychology?........................... 17
    Defining Sport Psychology... 17
    Is Sport Psychology Only for Athletes?....................... 18
    How Does Sport Psychology Help Me "Get into the Zone"? 19

Chapter 3: How Do People Get "into the Zone"? 22
    Overview of Techniques Used..................................... 22
    Active Awareness... 23

 Different Stages of Active Awareness: 24

 Techniques to Help with Active Awareness: 27

 The Power of Positive Rituals 28

 Attentional Skills 30

 Improving Your Attentional Skills 32

 Energy Management 38

Chapter 4: A Picture is Worth a Thousand Words 44

 What is Imagery? 44

 Why Should I Use Imagery? 45

 Problems in the Projection Room 46

 Timing and Detail in Imagery 48

 When and Where Should I Use Imagery? 48

 Final Tips on Imagery 51

Chapter 5: Creating a Way of Being 53

 Will the Skills I Learn Just Apply to Athletics or Work? 53

 How Often Will I Need to Practice the Skills and Techniques Learned? 54

 How Long Until I Will be Done Working on the Mental Side of Performance? 56

Chapter 6: I Want More Self Confidence, How Do I Get It? 58

    Defining Self Confidence... 58

    Cause or Effect? 61

    Once I Perform Better Then I Will Have More Confidence, Right? 62

Chapter 7: How Long Until I See Results?..................... 63

    The Key to Getting Results is You! 63

    This is a Journey not a Race 64

    Embrace the Journey... 65

Conclusion.. 67

Bonus Chapter: As a Parent How Can I Help My Athletic Child?... 69

    Learn to Ignite Their Own Self-development.............. 69

    The Importance of Intrinsic Motivation 71

    What I Can do Before and After an Athletic Competition 72

    All it Takes Sometimes is a Simple Question.............. 73

Book Resources... 75

Resources for your Body 77

Dedicated to . . .

There are so many people who have made this book possible. Every experience and person who has been in my life has had a hand in shaping who I am today and thus also played a part in this book coming to life. I have always been characterized as a very quiet person, finding it easier to express myself through words, and it became apparent very early on, that while my grammar and spelling were not the best, I had an ability to allow my thoughts to flow on paper with ease. While this gift is natural for me, I owe my confidence and recognition of this gift to my Grandma A. She too had a way with words and it is through working with her on all my poetry during grade school that I began to enjoy writing, and knew it was something I might like to do one day. So Grandma you are the first person I want to dedicate this book to, thank you for all your support, encouragement and guidance.

Next, I want to thank my Aunt Eleanor, she tirelessly proofread every single paper I wrote in graduate school, and helped me proof read and shape this book. Thank you so much for encouraging me, and reading through every word and sentence I wrote for school and for this book to help me create the best finished product I could.

To my parents thank you for your support over the years, for taking me to all my games and practices, getting me the best education possible and the extra tutoring that I needed to help me discover the ability I had, that was being overshadowed by my learning disability. Without all that extra help I wouldn't be where I am today. Mom, thank you for being my typing hands before I could type my papers in school, I would have had a few issues with my teachers if it wasn't for you. Dad, thank you for supporting me through graduate school, drilling me prior to tests and exams when I was a kid, and being my first proofreader. I am glad Aunt Eleanor didn't mind taking over for you, after I burnt you out during high school and undergrad!

Next, I want to acknowledge and dedicate this book to a person who has had a major influence in my life, and while it has been 12 years since he passed he still influences me on a regular basis. David McMaster, it is hard to put into words what you have meant to my life, you were far more than just my coach. You believed in me in a way no one else did in a time when many people didn't understand my decisions. Your words of encouragement and attitude towards life have been a pillar for me in making some of the biggest decisions of my life. Most importantly, you showed me how to take myself and my talent seriously, so thank you, as you played a major role in me being where I am today and for having written a book.

Finally, to my siblings, thank you for making me laugh and keeping things light and fun, during some of the most stressful times in my life. Every time I see you both I get a breath of fresh air and a renewed energy. You both have always been there for me, and while I am the odd ball out, you both make me feel comfortable and proud to strive for all my dreams. Thank you for being the best siblings I could ask for!

Foreword

Have you ever noticed the number of 'feel-good' stories in professional sports? You know, the ones where an undrafted or unknown player rises from the ashes of a broken past or distinct hardship to gain prominence, success, and respect. What about the number of high-profile athletes who become "busts"? Broke, destitute, or in trouble with the law? What's the difference between these two types of athletes, these two types of stories?

The difference lies in the makeup of each of their mental strength, and their ability to get in the zone. In a business that pokes and prods to find the most physically gifted athletes on the planet, it is the muscle between the ears that ultimately determines the success or failure of an athlete.

This book, by successful Sports Psychology Consultant Kate Allgood, provides the necessary link between physical and mental prowess in athletics and the ultimate success derived from it that so many athletes are missing. Allgood takes that fleeting phantom feeling of "being in the zone" that all of us athletes experience at one moment or another, and makes it concrete, real, and permanent. Her book does more than just define "the zone" needed for success in athletics, and more importantly, life, but gives practical working examples of how each of us can learn to identify, practice actual techniques, and achieve permanent success in reaching "the zone" and benefiting from it.

Allgood's book is for the professional and amateur athlete alike. For current and former athletes. For the young athletes first learning to tie their shoes and the veteran athletes long past their prime. This book is for more than athletes. It is for coaches, parents, family, friends, business people, and anyone else who is looking for a practical approach to building long-lasting mental and emotional strength, confidence, focus, and the ability to "get into the zone" in order to achieve each and every one of life's goals.

Brian Hannula, "NFLPA Certified Contract Advisor and Director at Alliance Sports Management Group"

Introduction

You will become clever through your mistakes
— German Proverb

WHO I AM

Beginning at a very young age my life has always been about performing at a high level. No matter the task I wanted to perfect it, so long as I was interested in it! This usually took me into the world of sports, where very quickly it became clear I was a natural athlete. Put a ball, bat, racquet or hockey stick in my hand and I used it in a far better way than most kids my age, male or female. The world of sports gave me a sense of delight and joy that nothing else could, and my natural talents took me far, the rest was covered by hard work.

My natural abilities served me well for most of my life playing competitive sports, but it was not without its hiccups. At the age of seventeen I started to feel the first signs of burnout, my primary sport of choice was hockey and I no longer loved going to the rink. I found myself wishing the time away while playing the sport that in the past my parents could not pull me away from. This led me to taking two years off from competitive hockey. At a time when my peers were selecting

Introduction

and playing for the university of their choice, I shifted my focus to academics and just being a teenager, instead of being the top level hockey player who had been offered scholarships from some of the best schools in the United States.

Walking away from a sport that had given me so much was not easy. My entire identity was wrapped around a game, and when it was gone, I had no idea who I was. Not knowing who you are is a scary thing, and can lead to some less than healthy behaviors. However, I was lucky enough to come across a professional who was able to help me find my way back and discover who I was without the game. It didn't happen over night, and it could be argued I am still in the process of self discovery, but what I discovered along the way shaped the direction I have chosen to take my life.

Once I stepped back, the pressure and need to be perfect eased with time, and I found myself loving the game once again. The desire to play for a NCAA Division I Women's Hockey program came back, and I began to put things into place to make it a reality. It didn't take long for the pieces to come together and within a few months I was offered a scholarship to a Division I program, where I ended up being captain and co-MVP for the year.

The rest of my time in university took me back to Canada, where I played my remaining three years at a Canadian university not far from my hometown of Toronto, Ontario. This allowed me to continue on my hockey path while still getting the support needed to excel not only in my sport but in life. I was fortunate to make some great accomplishments during my time in university. I was recognized as one of the best female athletes in all of Canada, and was pegged as a potential player for the 2010 winter Olympics to be held in Canada.

One of my discoveries during this time is that once the expectations of being the best, and possibly playing for my country, came back into focus the problems that had arisen when I was a 17 year old came back. The game became less fun, it felt like work, and my identity was again wrapped up in a game.

The six years of my life in which I went from burnout, to loving the game, and back to burnout, are what have taken me down this path of helping others to not only achieve a high level of performance but to do so while keeping the fun and joy alive, to find a more holistic and well rounded approach.

WHY I'M WRITING THIS BOOK

If you talk to athletes who played Division I sports, many of them will tell you how hard it was, not just physically, but emotionally and mentally. Many of my friends who played Division I hockey either stepped away completely from the game or took some significant time off afterwards, because they no longer saw the fun and joy in the sport. It had been sucked out of them by the politics and approaches taken. While these are things that were not within our control, what I have discovered is that many of us were not mentally or emotionally prepared for playing at such a high level.

Physically we were all some of the best, but I was never once introduced to or spent any time on the mental aspects of high performance, as I was with the physical, tactical or technical aspects. This I believe is a big missing link, the mental development not only of young athletes but also of people in general.

I am writing this book because while people know the mind is a powerful thing, they spend very little time harnessing, and training their minds to their fullest potential. This in turn leads to the stress, and pressure seen in any high performing area, taking away the joy and fun that is needed for people to reach their highest potential.

I have begun to think that a large part of this is due to the lack of education in this area. The term, psychology, can have a rather negative connotation associated with it, so people might think that a psychologist will "psychoanalyze" them and dig into their childhood past. This book is to show you that learning to "get into the zone" is nothing like that, rather it is about focusing on positive and action-based topics that can help you to perform at your best.

CHALLENGES THAT I SEE IN THE WORLD OF SPORTS AND OTHER HIGH END PURSUITS

The world of sports is getting more and more competitive everyday. The young athletes I work with today have more pressure and stress associated with their sport than I did, and I only see it getting worse.

I have seen kids as young as ten years old getting to the point of burning out because they feel so much pressure. While most of the time the pressure comes from within the person, I see that it also stems from the top which refers to sports organizations that create the schedules and set the way things are done. Colleges are now starting to recruit some athletes as young as thirteen years old. While it is not uncommon, and something I experienced, for colleges to start to take notice of an athlete at that age, recently there has been a step up where kids are being heavily recruited and promised positions at schools. This can create a lot of pressure because kids feel the need to live up to the reasons they have been recruited at such a young age.

Kids today are also expected to play their sport, and only that sport, pretty much all year round. If they don't, often they will not make the team. While hockey was my primary sport, the one I was most competitive in and put the most time towards, it did not stop me from playing other sports, which ultimately helped me become a great hockey player.

This was because playing these other sports forced me to focus on more than just hockey. It also helped my body get stronger as I was training different muscles for each sport, which reduced my risk of injury.

Compassion and balance seem to be left out of the pursuit of excellence. Compassion from others toward the athletes and compassion of the athletes toward themselves are important support for the striving athletes. It is sometimes forgotten that athletes are people. If they are treated as such they will ultimately perform better, as they will feel understood and heard. My first year of playing college hockey my parents were going through a divorce and I lost my first grandparent. Throughout the process I felt like no one really cared what was happening to me personally, only how I performed on the ice. At one point I struggled with a decision to miss a couple games to spend more time with my grandfather before he passed away. In discussing my feelings with the coach, I was made to feel that missing the games would be a bad decision, that I would be letting down the team. I felt like I was being forced to play with no regard to how I was feeling. I decided not to play the two games. The coach yelled at me and told me that I was not being a good team leader. I was made to feel that my life did not matter outside of what I could do for the team. I ended up transferring from that school because of that experience. The team lost their captain and best player as a result.

Interestingly enough, a couple years later at my new school a very similar situation came up again. One of my grandmothers passed away and the memorial was set for the same weekend as two huge games for the team. Once again I struggled with the decision to play or not. My coach and the captain of the team were completely understanding and compassionate towards me and the possibility of missing the two games. Because of the compassion they showed, I felt more loyalty towards the team, and decided to stay and play the games.

Living a balanced life is also healthy. As I tell many of my clients, when I was a child I took four months off from hockey every single year, and just got to be a kid. Some of them look at me with eyes wide open and gasp, "you took four months off!?" they say in disbelief, as they cannot comprehend doing that themselves.

Western society has developed the frame of mind that more work is better, and that quantity is better than quality. In order for someone to reach the top it is better to work harder than smarter. While hard work is necessary, there is such a thing as working too hard. A more balanced and well-rounded approach in the end would actually benefit people more in reaching their goals than simply working themselves into the ground.

An example I like to use to illustrate the importance of a good work to rest ratio is that of a muscle. In order for people to strengthen their muscles they need to work hard, but there is a fine balance between working hard and getting positive results and overworking. In order for a muscle to get stronger it needs to rest. The proper balance between working the muscle and resting it is what allows it to get strong, along with proper nutrition. If a muscle is overworked it gets weaker. For this reason I often tell my clients to approach life like athletes train. They work hard but they also rest a lot to prepare themselves to work hard again. We get the best results if we approach life as if we are training in intervals rather than running a marathon. A sprinter's body looks healthy and strong, a marathon runner's body looks weaker and less strong. There is nothing wrong with marathons, but our bodies and minds prefer sprints over long distances.

"Getting into the zone" requires people to not only work hard, but also to do so in a manner that works with their strengths, with enough energy and focus to perform within this state of consciousness during specific times. If one is too tired or burnt out then it becomes that much harder to "get into the zone" and "getting into the zone" is where the magic happens.

BARRIERS THAT I SEE IN CLIENTS THAT PREVENT THEM FROM "GETTING INTO THE ZONE"

The barriers that I see in my clients stem primarily from what I discussed in the last section. In society today, the pressure and stress to perform is massive, but this is not entirely the problem as pressure and stress are good to a degree, they are actually needed for growth. The problem and barrier for people is the inability to properly deal with the pressure and stress in their lives.

With proper techniques and strategies in place, the pressure and stress can be catalysts for people to reach their full potential. However, most people don't have any strategies or techniques in place, or if they do they might not be the right ones. Therefore, often, they simply make the situation worse.

Not many people can mention off the top of their heads three things they do on a daily basis that help them deal with the stress and pressure in their lives in a healthy manner. However, most people can tell you things they do to help with the stress and pressure that they know are not healthy for them, but give them some form of immediate relief.

The biggest barriers to "getting in the zone" and living a life that people want to live, is themselves. We make choices everyday that either help us or hinder us from reaching our potential. We are often so focused on the things we can't control that we forget about the things we can control, such as attitude, self-talk and our behaviors.

By exploring and discovering who we really are, detaching from the world around us and the messages it sends, we can begin to unlock the potential within. From this place we can create and implement strategies and techniques that are in line with who we are that will take us to a whole new level of performance!

PURPOSE OF THE BOOK

The purpose of this book is to provide a guide to the world of high performance and "getting into the zone". There are no guarantees for "getting into the zone" there are only methods and techniques. These can be applied to help improve the likelihood that one will "get into the zone" and thus perform at a level far beyond that of normal day to day consciousness. Even if you don't "get into the zone" you will still find yourself performing at a higher level. Part of being a great athlete is finding a way to play well even when things are difficult, which is what the information and techniques in this book are designed to help with.

The chapters in this book are designed around topics that I use with my clients. I also address frequently asked questions to help people to become acquainted with the topic of mental performance and the importance it has not only on performing at a high level but also for living a life far beyond what one might have thought possible.

Chapter 1: What does "getting into the zone" mean?

You need a certain amount of tension to be able to go. On the other hand, if you are too far gone, you just go off the deep end, you lose control. So it is just being able to find that little narrow comfort zone.
— Steve Podborski

DEFINING "THE ZONE"

"The zone" is a term that was coined in the sports world to describe a state of consciousness that leads to an athlete's ultimate performance. Most people have heard of this term, and while it is mostly used within athletics the principles behind it can be transferred to many other activities.

In psychology this is called "flow", a concept developed by Mihaly Czikszentmihalyi, and is considered complete absorption in what one does. It is accompanied by a feeling of enjoyment in the process, energized focus and complete involvement. It is a state of being in which people are able to harness their emotions and align them with the task at hand, in service of performing and learning.

What Does "Getting into the Zone" Mean?

There are a number of factors that contribute to someone being able to achieve a state of flow, but two main factors as illustrated in the diagram below are the challenge of the task and the perceived skill one has for the task. If the challenge is low and one's perceived ability is low, one feels apathy. If the challenge is greater than one's perceived skill one gets anxiety. The magic happens when the challenge is high and one is confident in one's ability to meet the challenge.

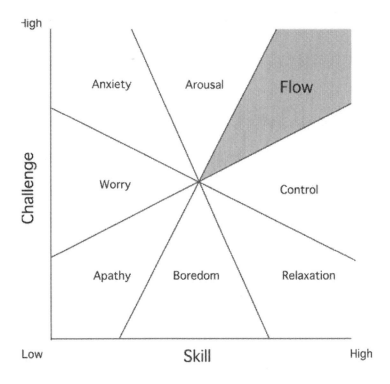

I remember the first time I became aware of this state of being, I was in my first year of playing college hockey and it occurred during my first game. I didn't realize I was in "the zone" until the next day, because when one is in "the zone" one truly can't be aware of the fact that one is in it. The awareness comes in a reflection process after the "flow" event. In hockey games, music is often played between the whistles. During my first game I didn't hear any music, that is how focused and in "the zone" I was. The next day in my second game of the weekend, I heard the music. I turned to a teammate to comment on how they hadn't played music the day before, well they had!

Of course after that point I kept trying to "get into the zone" again but as will be seen in a couple sections, it was not easy to do. Needless to say I have never played in a game again without hearing the music. This doesn't mean I didn't have moments of being "in the zone" during my games, but nothing that lasted an entire game. While I am sure I might have been in "the zone" before, this was the first awareness I had of a different state of consciousness while playing hockey.

THE BENEFITS OF "GETTING INTO THE ZONE"

Any person who has experienced being "in the zone" can tell you the benefits of being in that state of consciousness; you ultimately perform well beyond what is normal for you. It is as if you can do nothing wrong. You say all the right things, you make all the right decisions, and you make moves you have only dreamed of making in a highly competitive setting.

When you are "in the zone" you allow all the work, all your talent, skills, expertise, and knowledge to be on full display, in essence you get out of your own way. The number one thing that people struggle with is being in their own way when it comes to performing up to their potential. While you are "in the zone" that is no longer the case, your mind takes a backseat, and the flow of energy, focus, and knowledge takes over.

I have experienced being "in the zone" not only in sport but in school, while working on my Masters degree. One of the benefits of studying this type of topic is that one gets to experience it oneself, and in my case, the results were beyond amazing. My papers pretty much wrote themselves. Time and time again I was able to "get into the zone", where it felt at times like someone else was writing my papers, and I had no clue what was being written. However, when I reread my work, it all made sense and the language and tone used were far beyond what I had experienced in my writing in the past.

WHY IT IS HARD TO "GET INTO THE ZONE"

I think one of the hardest things for people regarding "getting in the zone" is that once they have been there they try to recreate it, and force themselves back into the same experience they had. Part of being "in the zone" is allowing things to flow, and most of the time people are trying to control how things look, instead of just letting things be and unfold naturally.

There is no way to predict exactly how being "in the zone" will look, and there are no guarantees about being able to get into it. All one can do is create an environment and way of doing things that increases the likelihood of it occurring. What I have found most useful is a routine of learning to simply let things go and allow things to occur as they are meant to.

This is what I did before each paper I wrote, and this is what I do before each game, and each day. To relinquish control is one of the hardest things to do, because we believe that the feeling of being in control will make things easier, that we will be able to predict outcomes and therefore things will be less unknown. This is far from the truth, and if one can learn to let things flow more freely, getting "into the zone" will become easier.

Another reason I feel that it is difficult lies in our perception of our own abilities and skills. As was seen in the diagram, there needs to be this perfect blend between the level of the challenge and the level of our perceived skill to take on the challenge. Confidence and self-esteem are often not where they need to be. This is why I see a lot of people's anxiety while I'm working with them. A lot of people see their abilities as less than they really are. This perception puts them in a state of anxiety which makes it difficult to get into a state of flow.

Chapter 2: What is sport psychology?

Athletes today need to balance the stressors of life with the stressors of his/her sport and be able to handle the pressures of success and of failures or temporary defeats and setbacks.

DEFINING SPORT PSYCHOLOGY

Sport psychology is concerned with understanding the "mental game", whether that game is athletic or otherwise. It is about human performance and building the necessary mental skills and techniques necessary to perform consistently and effectively regardless of the situation. Sport psychology is a discipline that investigates and seeks to understand the factors that are involved in reaching and consistently maintaining optimal performance—to strive to achieve one's best.

To help with understanding the role sport psychology plays, it can be helpful to ask yourself this question: "Are you performing at your very best with no room for improvement?" No one will ever answer this question affirmatively, most people will say there is a gap between how they are performing and how they are capable of performing. Sport psychology aims to create knowledge that will help close the gap between people's current level of performance and what they are capable of doing.

Most people spend the majority of their time working on the physical, technical or tactical elements of their professions or performances, with very little time and effort set aside to work on building their "mental muscles" and stamina. This is what most people call their "mental toughness". Everyone knows it exists, but very few people actually work to improve it.

In order to truly perform at one's optimal level, to reach the goals and level of performance one has set for oneself it is necessary to start looking at the mental side of performance. This is where sport psychology comes in. It is the area of study dedicated to training the mind.

IS SPORT PSYCHOLOGY ONLY FOR ATHLETES?

As you might have discovered as you have been reading this book, sport psychology is not just for athletes. Some people even understand it as more like performance psychology than sport psychology, as the principles are applicable to any arena of performance. The only thing that changes is the context with which one applies the information. Helping someone to perform under pressure, to get "into the zone" or learn to focus more effectively is the same in any arena of performance.

Most sport psychologists work both with athletes and individuals in business.

As I indicated above, I was easily able to apply the information learned about "getting into the zone" from my courses in sport psychology to my work in writing papers. I am applying them again as I write this. I have also worked with a number of individuals in sales and real estate, business executives, Navy Seals, doctors and lawyers to help them in the same way I have worked with athletes.

HOW DOES SPORT PSYCHOLOGY HELP ME "GET INTO THE ZONE"?

"Getting into the zone" is about a state of being. People often think that they can will themselves "into the zone" or make it happen whenever they want. Well this is not the case. In order to be able to "get into the zone" more effectively and consistently people must adopt a way of living that is in alignment with being able to more easily shift into the state of consciousness known as "the zone".

How this will be experienced will be slightly different for each person, as the idea is based around the premise of who one is, one's strengths, limitations and what works for one. However, in general, sport psychology helps people with "getting into the zone" because first it helps people to identify and know what their strengths are, what their limitations are and how pressure and stress will impact them. Once this is known then habits and routines can be created to allow someone to develop a state of being that is more inline with "getting into the zone".

Why are habits and routines important for "getting into the zone"? If one looks at the best athletes in the world they have put in place and follow routines, what some people might call superstitions, prior to each and every game, and even in their practice. The athletes are using their minds to create these routines and practices and to follow through on them. The mind is no different than any other muscle, it needs to be trained and warmed up so that it can perform optimally. Routines help with both aspects as you train your mind so that the particular ways you do things gear you up for the desired state of consciousness therefore getting ready for what you are about to do. In essence it is also warming up the mind as you would stretch or do light exercises with your body before a workout or competition.

It is amazing how many athletes don't have routines in place before a competition. More significantly they don't have routines and habits imbedded in their everyday life that are inline with how they want to perform. This is true in the business world as well, for example, most individuals don't have a set way of approaching a presentation or sale.

In order to more easily "get into the zone" people need to constantly prepare their minds for it. Some of the effective techniques will be discussed further in depth in later chapters.

Activities such as meditation, visualization, how one talks, thinks or walks and in general how one lives one's life from day to day are what will determine one's ability to "get into the zone" more consistently.

Chapter 3: How do people get "into the zone"?

We are what we repeatedly do.
Excellence, then, is not an act, but a habit.
— *Aristotle*

OVERVIEW OF TECHNIQUES USED

My approach starts by understanding where people want to end up. What are their goals and dreams? Then I investigate what they are doing on a day to day, week to week and month to month basis to get there. Most people have a long term goal, but don't have the smaller more manageable goals in place that line up with the end goal.

Next, we need to discover their strengths and limitations, and how these factors impact them the most under pressure. Understanding how people behave and experience themselves under pressure or stress is important in my view because the pressure can cause significant changes in their normal way of being. The ability to perform up to one's potential is often altered and this can have drastic effects on performance. Pressure situations can also reveal the barriers for people to "get into the zone". Are they going to over think the situation? Will they miss important information because they were too focused and had tunnel vision? Do they have the ability to see the big picture and all the information in front of them? All of this impacts focus and the ability to make effective decisions, and to be in the state of flow.

The following sections present different techniques and skills that people need to develop regardless of their strengths and limitations in order to more easily "get into the zone" and perform up to potential.

ACTIVE AWARENESS

This is the first skill that needs to be developed because without awareness you will not have the ability to make the necessary changes for improving your performance. For example, if you are not aware of how frequently your negative self talk is, there is no way for you to alter that pattern of thinking.

Active awareness requires us to notice what is happening immediately inside us and around us. Most people are unaware of their inner dimension - the way they tend to think, the images they have, all the nuances of their being that are products of their past and current experiences. For some, learning to become more aware will be more natural than for others, just like any skill that needs to be developed. I know for myself, this has been one of the hardest skills to develop.

When I first started the journey of my own personal growth, I was very unaware. As I became more and more aware, the difficulty no longer was being aware of my inner dimensions but changing them.

I have often thought of the path towards active awareness as a series of stages. As we move through these stages our active awareness develops and grows. The length of period each person spends in the different stages varies. I know for myself there have been times where I have spent years in one stage of awareness. To take years to develop a skill might seem long, but as you will discover throughout this book, developing our minds takes time. Patience for the rate in which you move through things is a must.

DIFFERENT STAGES OF ACTIVE AWARENESS:

Stage One:

In stage one we are unaware of our inner dimensions. We move through life with blinders on, and have difficulty seeing, for instance, our own anger and how it makes us act. For example, this is often seen when athletes start yelling at the referee or take bad penalties, in retaliation.

Stage Two:

We begin to become aware of our inner dimensions, but in retrospect. We see things after they have occurred. We see after our competition, how getting angry and taking action, impacted our own performance and that of the team. Often in this stage we will think "why in the world did I do that?"

Stage Three:

I think this is the most frustrating stage, as we become aware while we are doing something, without the ability to alter it. Using the example of getting angry at the referee or taking a bad penalty, we observe ourselves getting angry, and yelling or taking the penalty, and are aware that it might not be the best thing to do, but we have difficulty stopping ourselves from doing it.

Stage Four:

In this stage we now have more of an ability to be aware and change things in real time. We observe our anger rising, we feel a desire to yell at the referee or take the penalty, but we are able to stop ourselves from acting on our emotions. Often this occurs because the part of us that observes the anger, overrides the emotion, by seeing the consequences of acting on our emotions.

Stage Five:

This stage is about being proactive, and doing things regularly that help us to monitor our inner dimension and take action before we get to the boiling point, and fall into stage four. Using the anger example again, we become aware prior to our competition that we are a bit angry, and choose to do something then to help release the anger before the competition. By releasing the anger, we no longer have it built up inside of us. With less anger built up, we are less likely to become overly angry during our competition and the situation that made us want to yell at the referee, it no longer has such a dramatic impact on us.

As can be seen through the different stages above, one of the key elements in active awareness is learning to become an observer and separate from our inner dimension. Everyday we get messages, from our body, mind and feelings. However, we are so attached to them, that we allow them to be our reality. We allow our body, mind and feelings to tell us who we are and how we are going to perform.

We are distinct from our body, mind and feelings. We can observe our physical body, by listening to the physical sensations telling us how strong, tired or healthy we are. We can also go within ourselves and observe what type of emotions we are feeling. We can feel anger, sadness, joy and happiness. Feelings change radically from moment to moment, which is important to remember, because who we are does not change radically from one moment to the next. Finally, we are also distinct from our minds, we can "see" and "hear" our thoughts. We can tell ourselves to focus better or stop worrying, but often our minds don't listen.

As we tune in more and more to the observer within all of us, we learn to become more and more aware of our inner dimensions, which allows us to make choices. It can be thought of as a center of "pure awareness". Each of us can move to a place within ourselves where we can observe what is happening at the mind/body/feeling level and remain unshaken by it. This position of observing, but not being dominated by our inner state frees us to take the action we choose to take. Otherwise our anger, for example, might determine how we act, rather than our choosing how we want to respond. From that observer place of "pure awareness" we can choose to actively work with our awareness.

TECHNIQUES TO HELP WITH ACTIVE AWARENESS:

These two techniques are designed to help with active awareness by seeing things in a different light than what we are currently experiencing.

1. Physical Movement

Some people, when they are unhappy with what is happening to them, will physically move to get a new perspective on the situation, for example, go for a walk or run. By doing this they can look back to the spot they were just in and talk to themselves like this: " Well, Kate, you're really getting upset over that, aren't you? Is it really worth it? What is really important here?" Physically, and emotionally, you move into a position where you are in charge again, as opposed to letting your anger and racing mind take charge.

2. Reframing

Reframing is a technique that allows you to take a situation and look at it in a new way that is less threatening. For instance, I used to really get bothered by coaches who yelled. However, once I reframed the situation to look at the yelling in a more comical, light hearted way, it became easier to hear the underlying message, and not take the yelling as personally. This then allowed me to respond by stepping up my game. I still would prefer a coach didn't yell, but it is important that when you are put into a situation that is not optimal, you find a way to view it in a way that benefits you.

These are just two of many techniques that can be used for developing active awareness. Remember that there is no right or wrong way, only what works for you. So become creative and find a solution that will help you to become more aware, dis-identify with your current situation and move into a place of being calm and centered, so that you do not let the situation around you negatively impact your performance.

THE POWER OF POSITIVE RITUALS

Everyone knows that athletes can be superstitious, and while superstitions and rituals can at times look very similar the underlying mechanisms and processes behind them are very different. Superstitions give your power to something outside of yourself. When I was a kid I would not re-tape my stick until I stopped scoring. There were times when the tape on my stick would be shredded and could use a re-taping but because I believed it had something to do with my scoring I wouldn't change it. In this instance I gave my power to some hockey tape, rather than understanding it had nothing to do with my ability to score.

Rituals, on the other hand, are a systematic way of doing things that set you up to be more successful and focus on what you need to do instead of being distracted. While they can be important elements in high performance, as long as you do not give them all the power, then they can greatly benefit you.

So what does it mean to develop positive rituals? Well, rituals are not only for sports but for all facets of life. Each person reading this has a certain ritual for brushing their teeth. You do it when you wake up, or after breakfast, and right after dinner or before bed. You have created positive rituals around this necessary part of your oral and overall health.

The rituals for performance are no different. From creating rituals about the food you eat, when you go to the gym, and when you take mental rest times, everything in your life can become a positive ritual for your success. The people who are able to maintain a healthy way of eating do so because they have created rituals around food. While sometimes this means a lack of creativity or eating very similar things, they are able to stick with eating healthily compared to those people who don't.

For athletes, if you create one ritual and one alone, make sure you do so around your performance. Pre-performance routines are essential for success, and yet many athletes don't have them. Know the best ways to get yourself mentally and physically prepared and make sure you follow that positive ritual every time. As mentioned before make sure not to attach or give so much power to the ritual that if you happen to need to miss doing it or adjust to it you can't perform. So having a plan B or shorter ritual is always helpful for being prepared. A ritual that is done routinely and consistently over time will still have a positive effect even if you miss it once in a while.

ATTENTIONAL SKILLS

Perhaps no other area of performance captures the attention of individuals more than attentional skills. On the surface the concept of attention appears to be something of a contradiction. It can be experienced as positive or negative depending upon the circumstances. You are paying attention when you're daydreaming and if your intention is to do some creative problem solving it is positive. However, if you're in the middle of a competition, you've got the wrong attentional focus.

Every form of attention has its place. The key, as we shall see, is the congruency between the demands of the situation and the attentional style you bring to it. One of the major problems for Olympic athletes who do not perform at their expected level is that they are "blown away" by distractions. Athletes are usually prepared for the physical performance, but they are sometimes not prepared for the multitude of distractions they have to face in competitions. Their focus is everywhere, not on the task at hand.

There are three main types of attentional skills that I look at with clients, they are analytical, awareness and focus or follow through. Every person has these three attention styles, but one is usually more developed than the other two and one is under developed compared to the other two.

Depending on the demands of the situation people will utilize one of these three attentional styles to effectively accomplish a task. The problem occurs when the attentional style that one is using and the demands of a situation do not match up. A great example in athletics occurs when athletes are trying to shoot a ball. Instead of focusing on simply shooting the ball they are analyzing all the potential ways it could go wrong or all the options they may have.

There are a couple reasons why this can occur, one is stress, another is athletes who take their everyday attentional style into a situation that does not mesh with the specifics of the situation. The example above is often seen when student athletes, who are very good analytical thinkers, take this frame of thinking into their sport. They are so adept at the analytical style that they don't react quickly enough to move out of this style when necessary. School provides more than enough time for projects and papers to be done and handed in. However, this time frame doesn't train and teach the athletes how to react quickly within sports, and moving from one style to the next. People need to learn to move from one attentional style to another depending upon the situation.

Stress impacts our ability to shift attention styles effectively, because as stress and pressure increase we often automatically go to our favorite attentional style. We then get stuck there, and unless the situation demands that particular attentional style then we can get into trouble. For example, a quarterback who needs to have a high level of awareness as he receives the ball and see all his options could get into trouble if he is too highly focused. He could miss a wider span of information that is important not only to throw to the appropriate player but also to avoid getting sacked.

IMPROVING YOUR ATTENTIONAL SKILLS

Sport psychology is a discipline that focusses on planning and creating options to help with the mental aspects of peak performance. Improving attentional skills is part of that. At my office in San Diego these are some of the skills I implement with my clients on a regular basis to help them improve their attentional skills.

1. Design the event out

Designing the event out means to look throughly at the event and figure out what you are going to do. How are you going to prepare? What possible distractions will there be and how will you deal with them? What do you need to pay special attention to? What are the keys to your success in this situation?

It is important for athletes to think about an event beforehand, and see what could take them away from being "in the zone" and performing at a high level. While you do not want to overly focus on potential negative situations, it is important to have a plan in place. Unexpected things happen all the time during competitions, and if you don't have a plan in place for how to deal with situations, that can make things worse. If you have a plan in place, it often makes it easier to stay focused and regroup from something unexpected. Sometimes simply acknowledging that everything might not go according to "plan" is enough, because it helps to increase the awareness of the athlete prior to the competition.

I was working with a marathon runner for an upcoming race, and we had talked about a lot of different situations that could arise, and what she would do if they did. One thing we didn't talk about was the weather, as the race was in California, and we both expected it to be nice, as that was what was predicted. The morning of the race it turned out to be very cold, and she was unprepared both mentally for the cold but also hadn't packed cold weather running clothes, which made it worse. This was a lesson to both of us, that it is important to not assume anything and look at even the most outrageous circumstance that might occur. Of course the next race, we went over the different scenarios for the weather, which helped her a lot, as her next race the weather was not as it was predicted to be either.

Planning for distractions

Distractions are one of the main things an athlete needs to plan for. It is necessary to have a series of skills you can call upon to refocus your attention when you find yourself distracted.

If you are a high performer you most likely have a distraction plan. A distraction plan is knowing what potential distractions exist in your performance arena. It is also knowing what you will do if you get "hooked" by a distraction to bring your focus back to where it needs to be. If you don't have a distraction plan, then the following information is a "must read". Distraction plans are an integral part of the work that needs to be put in place, in order for athletes to perform at the levels they are capable of. Planning for distractions is not enough, it is also important that once the work is planned you then put that plan into action.

As mentioned earlier it is important to not have blinders on when you go into an event, but also it is important that you are not too aware as to get distracted. Once you have identified potential distractors, then you need to have the necessary skills and tools available to help with anything that could pull you away from what needs to get done and staying focused. Possible distractors such as negative thoughts, or the event running behind, can impact even the best performers if they are not prepared and have a plan in place.

2. Develop a strategy

Once you have designed the event out then the work is about developing strategies for the different circumstances that were identified. The idea behind developing a strategy is becoming aware, making a choice about what is best to implement in the situation and then acting on that strategy.

Reframing is a good example for this step. For instance, maybe you identified in step one that being unusually tired is a possibility. Often people will interpret this as a bad thing. However, this can be reframed to be seen as an advantage rather than a disadvantage. Being more tired will allow you to be more relaxed and calmer. Control will be easier. Seeing your tiredness in a positive light as an opportunity to relax and recharge will give you more energy in the end. Reframing is important for helping you stay on track.

Just the other day I used this strategy to my advantage. I was playing hockey, and after my first few shifts of the game, I could tell my body and mind were more tired than usual. In the past I would have just accepted this and let it negatively impact me, but instead, I reframed the situation and decided to believe that each shift I played I gained more energy. By the time the third period came around, I felt more like myself. This not only allowed me to feel better, but helped me maintain the focus I needed to play, while not feeling as energetic as usual.

The mind can be like an untrained horse; it can easily wander everywhere, and the more it gets used to wandering the more it will wander. It is important to learn to control your attention, from the minor situations to the bigger events. The more the mind gets used to maintaining focus, the easier it will be. There are several ways in which you can learn to control your attention.

Concentration control

Here are a few techniques to develop and improve concentration:

a. **Handling situation overload**: When you find yourself totally overloaded, try any one of these techniques:

- Change your environment. Find a quiet place to concentrate.
- Screen out the irrelevant, change seats, remove unnecessary distractions from your field of vision.
- Practice some deep relaxed breathing or meditation to calm yourself.

b. **Tuning in/Tuning out**: Read a book, or play a video game while music is on. Alternate your attention between listening and reading every 20 seconds. Try and become oblivious to what you are reading while you are listening and vice versa. Do this for about five minutes a day until you reach your objective of being able to completely block out one stimulus while concentrating on the other.

Another exercise for learning to tune in and out is, if several people are talking to you, to try and listen to just one person, and block out the rest.

c. **Juggling**: I think juggling is a great exercise for many reasons. It helps with coordination but it also can help with concentration. Juggling requires you to maintain a high level of focus in order for you to continue to juggle. It is also an exercise that can be easily made more difficult by the number of balls you are juggling or tricks you try and do, with each one requiring a new level of concentration.

d. **Become a detective**: Sometimes we have difficulty concentrating when something is dull or boring. When this occurs it is a great opportunity to use your imagination to create a story around the exercise with a beginning and an end. Looking at things differently helps with this. Become a detective. Ask yourself, how can I make this more exciting?

ENERGY MANAGEMENT

Managing energy, not time, is the key to high performance. Much of energy management has to do with the perception we bring to events and how we manage our attentional focus. There is no question that the "hurry-up" offence mentality of Western society encourages energy mismanagement and distorted values.

If you are stuck in traffic, do you put your car in neutral and push the gas halfway to the floor? Not likely. You wouldn't waste the energy (gasoline), and you wouldn't want to damage the engine of the car. Yet how many of us stuck in that same metaphorical traffic jam put our inner gas pedal halfway to the floor, thereby wasting our energy and damaging a much more important engine, our body, despite the fact that we can go nowhere.

Many people spend their energy trying to manage their time, however, time is not something we have much control over. However, how we use the energy we have is something we have control over.

How will you know if you are mismanaging your energy? Going back to the section on active awareness, we can can learn to observe the messages we are getting from our body and mind.

1. Physical symptoms: Such as rashes, sore backs, manifest themselves
2. Emotional symptoms: We become mired in negative feelings, pent up emotions
3. Behavior symptoms: We lose patience or speak too quickly

Every person will be different in terms of where they get signals that they are mismanaging their energy. For some people, it may be that they get a sore back, for others, they lose their patience. Regardless, they are all signs that we are mismanaging our energy. Often we try and treat it by fixing the symptom rather than going deeper and finding the real cause.

Here are a couple tips on helping with energy management and dealing with the stress in your life.

1. Acting as if you have time

The self-talk we repeat over and over to ourselves and that puts pressure and constraints upon us - or in other words, our general assumptions about life - leads directly to energy mismanagement. One subject that we frequently develop distorted assumptions about is time. Many people have the belief that there is simply not enough time to get everything done, that there is a constant time pressure.

This belief deeply influences our general, everyday, getting through life stress level. The more stressed we are the faster time will seem to go, and the more we do things that actually slow us down. We all do it when, we are running late, we forget where we put the keys or left our homework. We often forget something and have to double back to get it. So if we replace the belief system we have around time we can actually gain more time by slowing it down.

To understand how this occurs, we need to distinguish between chronological (the clock on the wall) and psychological (our perception of time) time. We don't have control over chronological time, an hour will go by regardless of what we do and it is always 60 minutes. However, we have control over psychological time, and can dramatically slow it down by choosing to believe and behave as if we have plenty of time. We acquire time by choosing at the mind, body and feeling levels that will enable us to act as if there is ample time at our disposal.

What we feel at one time is an accumulation of all the various places on which we are focusing our attention. We are often thinking about the present, past, and future all at once. Our attention is split into different directions of time, which increases our stress levels, our pace of life, and we begin to feel as if we do not have all the time we need to get things done right now.

Learning to be present and act as if you have time, is not only good for your health but also for your performance. When discussing their tennis match, hockey game or a great football catch, elite performers constantly make reference to their perception of time at that moment. While the game seems to go by fast, when they think back to any point in the game, it is as if everything was happening in slow motion.

To understand how this works, it is important first to know that a number of years ago psychologists discovered that we can hold seven pieces of information, plus or minus two, at any one time in our mind. This is one of the reasons why phone numbers are seven digits long. Think of the seven pieces of information as a film loop in which there is a bit of information in each of its seven frames. If four of the frames are focused on what you are doing now, and three are focused on other things, that film loop has to move very quickly in order for you to maintain a clear picture of the four frames you wish to concentrate on. However, if all seven frames contain the same information, you are truly focused on what you are doing; you are truly present in the moment. The film can then move slowly in order to project a clear image of what you are doing, which brings in the perception that time has slowed down.

2. Humor

Humor is a wonderful tool in helping us to manage our energy. A well timed joke can cut through any tension or feelings of hopelessness. It is important to not take ourselves or a situation too seriously. As I mentioned earlier with reframing the situation of a coach yelling, as soon as I saw the lighter side of the situation it became quite funny, and helped to cut through the stress that the yelling was creating. Watching a coach try and kick a hockey bag only to get it stuck on his foot, or throw a piece of chalk and have it hit him in the head, made for some fun entertainment.

Humor and playfulness are important factors for high performance. Whether around others or with ourselves the more we can see the humor in situations the better off we will be. Some of those opportunities to find humor will come when you notice you are mismanaging your energy, which will come in many different ways.

3. Managing your focus

I would say that focus is one of the areas where athletes mismanage their energy the most. This leads to a decrease in performance. In order to stay focused we cannot maintain a highly concentrated intensity over a long period of time. The more intense our focus the shorter we can maintain it. Our minds and bodies need to pause and relax in between periods of intense focus. As mentioned previously think of a sprinter versus a marathoner.

We have to fit in breaks and teach our bodies and minds how to go back and forth from being highly focused to taking a break and then back again. For example, hockey goalies can not concentrate 100% of the time, they will mentally fatigue and increase the chances of making mistakes. The goalies take a mental break when the puck is at the other end of the ice. They don't fall asleep and lose all focus, but they reduce the intensity enough to give themselves a break. Then when the puck comes back towards their end they can effectively focus and keep the intensity needed.

Being able to be relaxed and yet at the same time be highly focused is a skill that needs to be developed. More experienced players are able to maintain a higher level of focused attention for a longer period of time than their less experienced counterparts. They have learned how to use their attentional skills flexibly and appropriately. When athletes make more errors in the second half of a game, it is often not due to physical fitness, which is easily tested, but often due to the fact that they are not concentrating to the extent that they were earlier. This could be because they burned themselves out in the first half or need some additional skills that will allow them to narrow their attention and stay focused at the appropriate times in the second half.

Chapter 4: A Picture is Worth a Thousand Words

Imagination is more important then knowledge
— Albert Einstein

WHAT IS IMAGERY?

Imagery is one of the most powerful tools that I use while working with clients. As the title of this chapter says, a picture is worth a thousand words. Many people try and think their way through things, rather than creating a picture of what they want. Imagery is able to help clarify within your own mind what you want and how you want it to look.

Imagery is not only about creating pictures in your mind. Many people believe that in order to do imagery or have success with it you have to be able to create these very detailed images. However, imagery is more than just pictures, it is about involving all of your senses, taste, touch, smell, feeling, sight and noises. Each person will have senses, much like attention skills, that are more developed, and these are the senses we want to incorporate more strongly.

When I guide some people through imagery they do not pick up much in terms of what they see. However, they can feel themselves going through the motions, or can hear the sounds, or the smells of the location they are in. It is important when working with imagery to make it work for you and cater to your strengths. No two people will imagine things the same way, so just because you don't see pictures doesn't mean you are not capable of using imagery and benefiting from it.

WHY SHOULD I USE IMAGERY?

To understand why you should use imagery I want to first talk to you about how we all learn new things, especially physical things. When we are young and first learning to walk, we learn by observing others. From there we give it a try and figure out from falling how to balance ourselves and move forward. We are not instructed to put 70% of our weight on the front leg, and bend 30 degrees. If that was the case it would take us all a lot longer to learn the simple skill of walking. We learn by doing—holistically.

This way of learning is not exclusive to just walking. Kids learn everything "by doing", from throwing a ball to swinging a bat. Somewhere along the way though we begin to try and learn through verbal instruction. This makes everything harder, as our bodies do not understand words. Our bodies understand images in any form. So when we try and verbally communicate with ourselves there is a disconnect that makes things all the more challenging.

Imagery is important and beneficial to use because it opens up the channels for telling yourself what you want. There is also a biochemical change that occurs within the body during imagery, that creates the same neural connections formed by actually doing something. So by spending time doing some imagery your body not only thinks it is actually doing it, but you can imagine it exactly as you want, making it that much more powerful.

There have been numerous studies done, where one group does imagery and the other group physically performs the activity, such as free throws in basketball. Those that do the imagery turn out to do better in games with their free throw percentage than those who simply practiced them.

PROBLEMS IN THE PROJECTION ROOM

Sometimes when people are doing imagery, there is a gap in the film, or the picture gets hazy or turns upside down. There are a number of reasons this can occur. First, you might not have a clear intention as to how to proceed in that moment or you might be trying to do something you are just not completely comfortable doing at the moment. I will go over some tips on how to help below.

Sometimes during imagery people will get a sudden flash of falling, getting injured or making a terrible mistake. This is not an indication that these things will occur; sometimes it is your subconscious telling you to pay attention to a particular item or issue. Other times it might be a message to stick to your strategy and pay attention to what you are doing.

To help with any problems here are some tips to help:

1. **Clarify your intentions**: Make sure you are very clear about the fact you are doing an imagery exercise and why you are doing it.
2. **Relax**: Imagery is much more powerful the more relaxed you are. This is why hypnosis is often used and can be very powerful. Hypnosis is used simply to help people to relax to a greater degree than they might be able to on their own. In the hypnotic state you are more receptive to the images. This is true even without doing hypnosis, the more relaxed you are the more receptive you are.
3. **Use different types of imagery work**: There are two main scenarios that people will use with their imagery. One is actually doing the event and performing beautifully. Another is results imagery, that focuses on what people will see, and feel after having accomplished their intention.

TIMING AND DETAIL IN IMAGERY

I often get asked the question, how fast or slow should I make my imagery go? At first I was similar to many people and thought you should slow it down and create the imagery in slow motion. That way you could get all the details down, and it seemed to help with taking everything in. However, I discovered that the best timing for imagery is to experience it in the same time frame as it would actually take you to do the activity.

Imagery is an actual rehearsal, as far as the body is concerned. In order for imagery to be as effective as possible the time it takes to mentally go through something should sync up with how long it will take in real life. While I mentioned before that often people will try to slow things down, but when they actually try and do imagery work the problem is that things go too quickly. In this case adding more details will help with slowing things down.

WHEN AND WHERE SHOULD I USE IMAGERY?

Imagery is a great tool to use in many different situations. I will go over some of them here, but the list is not extensive but simply ideas and examples to help you see how it can be used.

Mental rehearsal:

I think this is the one most people think of when they think of imagery. Mentally preparing for something whether a sports event or a business meeting, allows people to understand how they will react to the situation, and to see themselves respond in a manner that lines up with the result they want.

Mental rehearsal and imagery is not about creating a fantasy. There has to be a real dose of reality within imagery in order for it to be effective. Seeing things that are not really possible isn't going to make them occur in real life. Mental rehearsal is about seeing yourself at the starting line of your race, chasing the puck, nailing the dive, etc. Taking in your emotions, the environment, how your body feels, and seeing how you react to what you are experiencing are the cornerstones of imagery.

This is the situation where you see yourself implementing strategies created for this moment, so that by the time you actually get to the event, you know what to do and what to expect. Nerves are natural but a lot of the time people will get more nervous because they feel nerves are something to worry about rather than knowing they are forms of energy that can be directed. You can still perform at a high level while nervous. We all have butterflies when we are starting to perform. The trick is not to try to get rid of them, the trick is to use your imagination and see them all flying in one direction toward your goal.

Relaxation and energizing:
Imagery is a great tool for helping with relaxation. It is one of the many ways I help my clients to relax prior to actually getting into the mental rehearsal part of the imagery. Everyone has a place that is relaxing to them, it can be real or imaginary. The important part is finding something that helps you to relax and bring down your arousal level.

For me this place is my family's cottage in Northern Ontario, Canada. It is one of the few places I feel completely at ease and detached from the world and all my responsibilities. If I am stressed out, I can take a few minutes to imagine myself at the end of the dock with my feet in the water looking out over the bay, and a wave of calm will come over me. This is also true of the sound of the leaves as the wind blows through them.

This technique is also useful if you need more energy. You can imagine how you want to feel at the end of the event, and maybe retrieve images from past performances where your energy level was where it needed to be. You can also imagine "parking" your feelings of fatigue and imagine increased focus and reacting to the challenge.

Often I will use a piece of advice I received a number of years ago to help with "parking" the emotions that are draining my energy. As you prepare for your event imagine taking off a coat with all your problems, fatigue or things that are interfering with your ability to be focused and energized and hanging it on a hook. The coat will be there when the event is finished, and you can put it back on afterwards, and then deal with what needs your attention.

Motivation:

Using imagery as motivation is about seeing what is possible. This has definitely become very trendy over the last few years, with what people call vision boards. People put images of what they want on a board and see themselves accomplishing or attaining what is on the board. This in turn motivates them to do the necessary work to get it.

I think this might be the type of imagery people use the most often today. We all want to see ourselves accomplishing or attaining desired outcomes or things, it helps to renew the motivation we have as it brings to the surface very strong feelings and emotions. I think if you combine this type of imagery with the others that I have mentioned, you will discover that the things you are striving towards will happen quicker and smoother.

FINAL TIPS ON IMAGERY

Imagery is an effective tool for helping you to get "into the zone" and accomplish great things, and to help you get the most out of your experience with it, here are some final tips to get you started.

Make sure you believe it can work or at least be willing to experiment with it. Hang up any skepticism you might have with your coat. If you do not believe it can work or if you are too skeptical it will be very difficult to drum up the emotions and sensations needed to enhance the experience. As you try it, make sure you use all your senses and bring in as much detail as possible. Like learning most skills, the more serious you take imagery work and the more you practice it the better you will become at it. If you create the time to implement imagery into your life it will become a powerful tool for you.

Some people also find it is helpful to keep written notes of their experiences. It is important to keep track of what works for you. Keeping a journal or notebook is a good way to preserve your experiences and see how you have progressed. Often people will start to drift away from what is working or forget over time what they did that worked. Using notes reminds you about what is the best approach for you. Finally, just do it. There is no right or wrong way, you have to start somewhere and the sooner you start the sooner you will understand how imagery works for you. Don't let not knowing stop you from implementing it, it doesn't have to be long, it could be 30 seconds but just start and keep at it.

Chapter 5: Creating a way of being

To live your life in your own way, to reach for the goals you have set for yourself, to be the you that you want to be—that is success.
— Terry Orlick

WILL THE SKILLS I LEARN JUST APPLY TO ATHLETICS?

I often get asked if the work I do with clients is just applicable to the world of athletics. This is far from the case. Everything that we do, including the techniques described in the last chapter are things that can be applied to all aspects of life. Helping someone to control their emotions is not just important in sports but also life.

I was working with a high school wrestler helping him with his emotions during his wrestling competitions. One day he walked in and started talking about how he was arguing with his parents, and was able to stop himself in the middle of it and to realize he was wrong. That type of awareness, control and ability to shift gears, was something he gained from learning how to do the same thing during wrestling. He learned a transferable skill.

The work that I do with my clients is not just about their sport or work. One cannot really box off different aspects of their life. If you want to be more confident in your ability to hit a jump shot, you have to also work on your confidence in other areas as well. Everything in one's life flows together, and more often than not, the problem seen in one's ability to get into "the zone" is due to a factor in another area of one's life.

Creating a way of being is how I help my clients to perform up to their potential. If you want to learn how to control your emotions then you need to learn to do so in everyday life, if you want to be more relaxed, then you need to create a way of being on a day to day basis that helps you to do so. You can't expect yourself to magically become a relaxed, calm and composed individual at a critical athletic moment if you can't do so day to day in less stressful or pressurized situations.

HOW OFTEN WILL I NEED TO PRACTICE THE SKILLS AND TECHNIQUES LEARNED?

How often do you practice anything you want to become good at? It is fascinating that while people understand that the mental side is important they spend very little time working on it. Yet they expect great, long lasting results even without the work. How long do you spend on the physical aspects of your sport? How long did you spend on your education?

Practicing the skills and techniques required to perform at a high level, should be done on a daily basis. It does not have to be a lot of work or time consuming, but everyday there are opportunities to practice. Whether it is practicing your breathing, managing your energy, visualizing little things in your life, or creating routines to help you be better every day, you can easily find ways to practice.

I have often had clients tell me that one of the difficulties they have with coming in to see me is that they can't find the time. They practice 6 days a week for a 2–3 hours a day on the physical side of their sport, and yet they can't find an hour to spend working on the mental side of things. These are the people who need it the most, but don't yet understand how powerful the mind is, and that one hour with me, will do more than the 2–3 hours they spend that day doing physical training.

The people I have worked with who excel, put in the work at the beginning with me, make sure to do the daily work required. Before they know it, they are seeing me less and less, and still getting better and better at the things we have been working on. The more dedicated people are in doing the work outside of our time together the quicker they will get the results they want and the more they will benefit from the time they have with me.

HOW LONG UNTIL I WILL BE DONE WORKING ON THE MENTAL SIDE OF PERFORMANCE?

If you want to continually grow and get better, then you will never be fully done. Just as professional athletes or super star business executives need to continually work on fine tuning their skills to perform up to a high level, the same is true for mental training. With all the changing circumstances and life situations you will face there is always more work that needs to be done.

Everyday brings new challenges and lessons to be learned, and it is because of this that we will constantly be tested and will constantly need to fine tune our mental skills. As soon as you think you have one skill down pat and you are finished needing to work at it, the farther you are from having truly mastered things. Those people who understand that this is an ongoing developmental process and they will never be finished learning and growing, the better they are at dealing with life's ups and downs.

If you think of life, in general, and skill building, in particular, as a journey, then you will understand that there is no real end point. No matter how much work you put in, how old you are, there is always more to learn and to develop. It definitely gets easier with practice, as you begin to understand how you react and process things. This knowledge will allow you to move through life much easier and quicker, but know that the work is still there.

Chapter 6: I Want More Self Confidence, How Do I Get It?

"Nobody can make you feel inferior without your consent."
— Eleanor Roosevelt

DEFINING SELF CONFIDENCE

I would say that self confidence is one of the most common topics I deal with when working with clients. Everyone wants more self confidence, and wants to know how to get it. To define self confidence I am going to use my experience of being truly confident within myself and also from what I have learned from dealing with others.

The first time I found out what true confidence was, I was twenty-two and nominated for an award. The award, which recognized the top four male and female athletes in all of Canada, took me to Calgary, Alberta and gave me the opportunity to hang out and be around other athletes from different sports who had also risen to the top. I spent quite a bit of time with one of the male athletes because we were from the same athletic conference and the organizing committee broke us up to do different events such as TV interviews based on our conferences.

Spending time with this individual allowed me to see what true confidence looked like. It was the first time I realized that true confidence borders very closely with cockiness or arrogance, but if one is astute one will see the difference between what is true and what is not. This athlete had gone up to his coach in his freshman year and told him that by the time he graduated the team would have won five championships (in Canada you can play college sports for five years). This could seem very arrogant, but this came from a place of true confidence in his abilities and skills.

He took what he had to offer seriously and wouldn't let anything take away from what he knew he could accomplish. He knew there would be tough times, and that things would not always go the way he had hoped, but it would not take away from his abilities and skills. The way he talked at times could seem arrogant, but it was true belief in himself and what he could do. I think at times projecting this confident image can make other people feel insecure and label the person as arrogant because they don't know that confidence within themselves.

This athlete, led his team to five straight championships, and created a dynasty for his school. Meeting him truly changed my life. As I have gotten older and taken my own skills and talents seriously, I have watched people become uncomfortable at times or feel I am being arrogant. So I do have to monitor my expressions and make sure that a line is not crossed, but it is also important for me to not let others shrink my confidence because they feel uncomfortable with it.

Some might ask how I knew this athlete was confident and not arrogant. Well at first I did think that he was arrogant, but once I got to know him, and really began to pay attention I noticed there was a difference. He had characteristics of being modest, humble and kind, in addition to having a high confidence in himself.

I see confidence as an unwavering belief in yourself, that is unshakable by circumstances or people around you. To take yourself seriously and know what you are capable of accomplishing doesn't mean that there won't be hardships or trials, but if you can still believe in yourself, in who you are and what you have to offer, then you are on your way to having good self confidence. It is being able to look at what the world is challenging you with and know that you are capable of meeting it head on.

When I step onto the ice and know that no one on the other team stands a chance against me I am there. Twice in college I experienced this feeling in overtime. I remember each time lining up for the face off, and thinking to myself how the other team didn't stand a chance against me, that I had an unfair advantage over them. I remember smiling and knowing that I would come out on top. Sounds pretty arrogant, I know, but both times I scored the winning goal, and knew that is the type of confidence that is necessary to succeed.

CAUSE OR EFFECT?

When clients come in for help with self confidence the first thing I tell them is we first need to understand if the issue is truly due to a lack of confidence or if there is something else going on that is impacting their ability to perform and is thus chipping away at their confidence. Depending on what we discover I use different approaches.

I am able to determine their confidence based on an assessment tool that every athlete takes while working with me, one of the characteristics being measured is confidence. Often what I see is that the confidence is good, but they are having a hard time shifting their attentional focus, which is impacting their ability to focus on the right thing at the right time and therefore, their level of performance. Over time this lack of focus does chip away at their confidence.

So at times confidence is the symptom of something else. This is where the level of confidence itself does not need work. Rather the athletes need help to develop better attentional skills so that they can perform up to potential. The confidence will take care of itself.

ONCE I PERFORM BETTER THEN I WILL HAVE MORE CONFIDENCE, RIGHT?

Playing and performing better will absolutely build confidence but this can be dangerous because if you rely on your performance to dictate your confidence level then your confidence will always be dictated both well and badly based on your performance. This will lead to a roller coaster ride of emotions. When you play well you will be happy, when you don't you will be upset, and your confidence will go along for the ride as well.

The goal is to have confidence regardless of how you play. True confidence as mentioned above is there regardless of the circumstances. Things are not always going to go your way, there will be tough times. However, if you trust yourself and your skills, and know that you can get through the difficulties, you will feel much better. When I ask athletes what they can do to help with their confidence, the first thing they usually say is play better. They are letting external factors dictate how they will feel. You must turn the tables and let your confidence dictate how you play.

Chapter 7: How long until I see results?

"Know yourself and you will win all battles."
— Lao Tzu

THE KEY TO GETTING RESULTS IS YOU!

I think that everyone knows to some degree that mental training is a process, but I still get asked the question all the time about how long will it take to see results, and what can someone expect. While I can give a general answer, and give examples of success, the ultimate determining factors are the individuals themselves. The biggest determining factor in the success of clients is their own commitment to the process.

Not only is commitment important, but those who truly understand that growing and changing is a process and can see the small successes are the ones who have the best results. People also have to be open enough for the change that is required to reach the level of performance that they are striving for. Often I find people stuck in their own way of doing things. While they come to see me for help they struggle with letting go, and sometimes they just can't seem to let go. In that case when they don't see instantaneous results, unfortunately they sometimes decide to stop.

Mental training is not for everyone. It requires great strength and determination to change and reach a new level of performance. Many people are comfortable where they are, and while they want change, they are not ready to let go of where they are. You are the creator of your own life, and while my job is to help guide you to a new level of performance, the driving force is you. I am only a guide, the information in this book is only a guide, what you do with the information is what will determine the results you will see.

THIS IS A JOURNEY NOT A RACE

Success and reaching your full potential is a journey, not a race. If you are always trying to get to a destination you will constantly be disappointed. We never stop growing, learning and developing as human beings until the day we die. Those who believe that they have reached a destination and are where they want to be, are farthest from it. Those who believe they still have lots to learn, are closer to reaching their full potential. Ask the experts in their field and they will tell you the more they know the more they feel they have a lot to learn.

This has probably been one of the most difficult concepts for me to embrace. There were many times in my growth when everything seemed good, and there will definitely be times when that is the case. These times can trick you into believing there is nothing left to learn. Then all of a sudden something happens, and you find yourself struggling with many of the same things you have in the past. The situation can even seem more difficult because it takes you by surprise, because you have convinced yourself you wouldn't have to deal with it again.

I think this was difficult for me because I thought there was an end point, and if I just reached it all would be good. It is only through understanding that life is a journey and that the goal is to learn and grow with each experience so that the next one is easier to deal with, that I learned the beauty of the journey, and stopped being so hard on myself.

EMBRACE THE JOURNEY

Our society is focussed on results and getting to a certain end point. We can think that when we get the new car, win the race or get the promotion then we will be happy. When you can learn to become happy with the process that it takes to get to those end results, then you will truly be happy, and your happiness won't be dependent on something external. When you find the joy in the small successes then life becomes fun and magical, rather than stressful and draining. Life is meant to be fun, but when we constantly see ourselves as not reaching our goals then life becomes more difficult.

How Long Until I See Results?

In the world of high performance, I often work with perfectionists, I know because I am one. The interesting thing I have discovered is that even if a goal is reached, for the perfectionists it is never good enough. They will convince themselves that the goal was not hard enough, and discount their accomplishment.

There are definitely milestones that can be reached and celebrated, such as winning a championship game, or graduating from school. These are things that should be celebrated, and are great markers in the journey of life. Embracing the journey is not only about its celebrations, and achieving great things, it is understanding that each accomplishment is a part of the journey. If your goal is to graduate from school, then accepting the journey is embracing all the joys and struggles that come along with that goal, and enjoying the time you spend in school, rather than becoming focused on what life will be like once you graduate.

Conclusion

The one thing over which you have absolute control is your own thoughts. It is this that puts you in a position to control your own destiny.
— *Paul G. Thomas*

Getting the most out of this book comes down to you. As mentioned in the last chapter, with this type of work the determining factor is the individual who is applying the information. This book is a guide to help you in understanding the world of sport psychology and getting "into the zone". What you do with the information is up to you. You can begin to apply the knowledge you have gained and work through the challenges that you will face, using what you have learned to help or you can decide that because it doesn't make everything all better the information isn't useful.

This book isn't going to make getting "into the zone" a piece of cake, or something that you can constantly achieve. It is designed to help you understand the underlying parts that exist to enable you to perform up to a high level, and to do so in a state of mind that makes the experience more enjoyable.

To get the most out this book you just need to start applying things to your life, see what happens, and make adjustments as you learn what works for you and what doesn't. This book is a starting point, and if you apply what you have learned and find yourself wanting more, then it might be time to look into finding someone to take you to that next level.

Bonus Chapter: As a parent how can I help my athletic child?

Education is not the filling of a pail, but the lighting of a fire.
— W.B. Yeats

LEARN TO IGNITE THEIR OWN SELF-DEVELOPMENT

While the number of studies that focus on how young athletes want their parents to behave before, during and after their sporting event, is still minimal, there are common elements starting to develop that are worth noting. In this section, I address this issue in order to begin to give parents a clearer idea of what their child is looking for from them. I am often asked by parents what they should do, and this section will go over many of the important things.

One of the first things that parents should be concerned about regarding their children is helping them to learn what is necessary for self development and growth. Often it is necessary for people to go through a crisis or some form of discomfort to reach a new level in their endeavor.

It is important that children understand this so that they can then learn to reframe the situation into one that works positively for them. Make sure though, that if time is needed before reframing can start, to give your child the time to mourn or vent the loss, change or hardship before moving onto reframing.

Sometimes children will be over-excitable, meaning they can have very strong feelings and emotional reactions to events. This can lead to them being labelled as "too" emotional, touchy, imaginative, or smart for their own good. It is important not to judge the children but to take these strong emotions and feelings and use them in a positive way to help with their development. Assure them that it is okay for them to feel this way, and they can use the energy beneath the emotions and apply it to some thing that they need to do. This is a great way for them to start to understand themselves, and how to use their emotions to their advantage.

Children need to learn to develop what is within them. All great performers have a strong bias towards self development. As a parent you are in a unique position to help your child to develop this from an early age. Your advice or attitude should focus on helping them unlock their own potential rather than telling them how their skill development should go or look. Those that have truly succeeded have always gone against the grain, and the more people begin to understand the benefits of their unique qualities the better equipped they will be for succeeding in life.

THE IMPORTANCE OF INTRINSIC MOTIVATION

As most people know it is much better for anyone to be motivated from within rather than some external reward or reinforcement. This is even more important in children. It is truly important to make sure that the reasons they are doing whatever it is they are doing is for "their" reasons and relates to their inner needs and satisfactions. They need to "own" what they are doing.

As parents this means being aware of the behaviors that you are rewarding and reinforcing. Let's take an example of a baseball player, who is up to bat. He puts in a lot of effort but at the same time throws his bat and helmet after striking out. If the coach or parents tell him "good effort, next time you will get it", they are not only reinforcing the hard work but also the helmet and bat throwing. So they need to distinguish between the behaviors that are positive and those that are negative in their feedback to their child, and only reinforce the positive ones.

I once had a client tell me that his parents were going to take him out for ice cream if his team won. While it may seem like an innocent gesture, to the boy it means that if you win you get something and if you lose you do not. This will take any intrinsic motivation that he might have and turn it into extrinsic, leading the boy to play for the reward rather than for himself and his own reasons. This in turn can lead to more pressure, and ultimately to him not having fun and even getting really down on himself.

So my advice is to choose very carefully what you say and do as to make sure you are not rewarding global behaviors or turning intrinsic motivation to extrinsic, because that is where problems will begin to develop.

WHAT I CAN DO BEFORE AND AFTER AN ATHLETIC COMPETITION

This section addresses some of the areas that parents ask most about. The behaviors parents exhibit can positively or negatively affect their child's level of confidence, anxiety, feelings of competence and motivation. Depending on the gender of the children, the parent who has the most influence on their sporting experience will usually be the parent of the same sex.

Children see their parents as able to help them enjoy and get the most out of their sporting experience when they behave in appropriate ways. This includes helping them physically and mentally get prepared prior to their competition. It means helping them with simple tasks such as taping ankles, preparing food and getting them to the venue on time. This is all children really want from their parents.

Once the competition starts children are looking for their parents to take a back seat and support the entire team.

Once the competition is done children want realistic feedback from their parents. This is important because your children need to believe in what you are saying. If the children feel they had a bad game and you say great job, they will begin to distrust your opinion and feedback.

Obviously it is important not to put them down, but let them have time to process on their own. What did they think of the game? Would they like any feedback from you? If they agree then give them an honest appraisal of their performance. They will appreciate this much more than a simple "good job!" They want to trust that you will tell them the truth. This way when you do say they had a good game they will be much more likely to take it in and believe it.

ALL IT TAKES SOMETIMES IS A SIMPLE QUESTION

Every child is different, and while the tips outlined in this chapter might work for your child, some might not. It is important to ask your children what they are looking for from you and what they need. Let your children begin to develop and understand for themselves what they need. It is important for the growth and development of their autonomy in life.

When I was child playing sports, I don't ever remember my parents asking me what I wanted or needed from them to support me. They just brought what they thought I needed to the table, and while sometimes it was accurate other times it was not, and it put more pressure and stress onto me than was necessary.

The first thing children don't want to hear after a competition is all the things they have done wrong or could improve upon. At the same time they do not want non-stop positive support. Let your children begin to develop their own abilities to break down the game and understand what they did well and what they could improve upon; if they need help let them know you are there to help them, but let that decision be up to them.

One final note, as a parent be very aware of what you say about other children on your child's team. If children hear parents talking about one child, they will begin to think that parents also talk about them, and this can lead to them starting to worry about what others think about them, instead of thinking about the task at hand.

As parents you are in a great position to help your children get the most out of their experience in sports. The experience they have will be there for the rest of their life, and if you can help create joy, happiness, and confidence through their sports, this will stick with them for the rest of their life, not only in sports but also in achieving goals in other areas of life.

Book Resources

This is a list of books that I have read and used to help me personally grow and gain more insight into the mental side of high performance. I also take this opportunity to give credit to the creator of the flow chart seen on page 27

Flow Chart
Flow: The psychology of optimal experience by Mihaly Csikszentmihalyi

In Pursuit of Excellence: How to win in sport and life through mental training by Terry Orlick

Blink: The power of thinking without thinking by Malcolm Gladwell

Outliers: The story of success by Malcolm Gladwell

The Inner Game of Tennis: The classic guide to the mental side of peak performance by W. Timothy Gallwey

The Speed of Trust: The one thing that changes everything by Stephen M.R. Covey

The Power of Habit: Why we do what we do in life and business by Charles Duhigg

Start With Why: How great leaders inspire everyone to take action by Simon Sinek

Biology of Belief: Unleashing the power of consciousness, matter and miracles by Bruce H. Lipton

Ignite the Third Factor: How do you get people committed to reaching their full potential? by Dr. Peter Jensen

The Power of Full Engagement: Managing energy, not time, is the key to high performance and personal renewal by Jim Loehr and Tony Schwartz

Resources for your Body

I want to take this opportunity to acknowledge that while the mind is powerful and has an impact on the physical performance of an athlete, an athlete also needs to make sure they are taking care of their body, and have a team of people whom they trust to help them through the physical challenges of their sport. I know personally the psychological implications injuries can play on an athlete, and the importance of finding modalities that can help. After years of using many different physical modalities, and understanding there are many more I have not used, the below list outlines my go to modalities and people who helped me recover from my athletic injuries and continue to keep my body functioning at the highest level!

If you live in the San Diego area I have listed the people I personally use, if you do not live in the San Diego area, I have also included websites for the modalities where appropriate so you can find someone in your area. You can also always feel free to contact me directly through www.qpathlete.com and I can connect with the professionals here to help find you someone in your area.

Muscle Activation Techniques:
Corporate Website: www.muscleactivation.com
Recommendation for San Diego:
Neuromuscular Fitness Training
Nicholas Linn
www.mynft.com
Email: nic@mynft.com
Tel: (619) 495-2100

Acupuncture:
Recommendations for San Diego:
Jacintha "Jaz" Roemer—JazHands Therapeutic Massage and Acupucture
Email: jacintha.roemer@gmail.com
Tel: (619) 721-7266
www.jazhandsmassageandacu.com

Chiropractic:
Recommendations for San Diego:
Family First Chiropractic & Wellness Center
Dr. Payton and Dr. Dawn
www.familychirosd.com
Email: info@familychirosd.com
Tel: (858) 279-1012

Elite Health
Dr. Pawn Dhokal
www.elitehealthpractice.com
Phone: (619) 301-8188

Massage Therapy:
Recommendations for San Diego:
Somasense Bodywork
Tina Thomsen
www.somasensebodywork.com
Tel: (360) 220-7155

BioHarmony
Brooke Sullivan-Brown
www.wellbeingbioharmony.com
Email: info@wellbeingbioharmony.com
Tel: (720) 404-3511

Naturopathic Doctor:
Stengler Center (Located in San Diego but also can work with those from a distance)
Dr. Mark Stenger
www.markstengler.com
Email: info@markstengler.com
Tel: (760) 274-2377

Athletic Supplements:
Advocare
www.advocare.com
Contact Person: Mitch Ryan
(209) 304-7642

Skoop
www.healthyskoop.com

Vega
www.myvega.com

Contact Information

I am always happy to help in anyway I can, so if you are in need of more advice or help being pointed in the right direction please feel free to give me a call directly and I will be happy to speak with you free of charge! Thank you so much for reading this book and starting your quest of training your mind.

Kate Allgood
wwwqpathlete.com
5752 Oberlin Dr Ste 223
San Diego, CA 92121
Phone: 619-446-6846

Made in the USA
San Bernardino, CA
28 July 2017